ISBN 978-0-260-45725-7
PIBN 10949474

Abraham Lincoln's Political Career through 1860

Ballots 1860

Excerpts from newspapers and other sources

From the files of the

Lincoln Financial Foundation Collection

FOR PRESIDENT, 1860

ABRAHAM LINCOLN,

OF ILLINOIS.

FOR VICE PRESIDENT,

HANNIBAL HAMLIN,

OF MAINE.

Electors at Large,

HON. JAMES POLLOCK.

HON. THOMAS M. HOWE.

1 Edward C. Knight,	13 Francis B Penniman,
2 Robert P King,	14 Ulysses Mercur,
3 Henry Bumm,	15 George Bressler,
4 Robert M Foust,	16 A. B. Sharp,
5 Nathan Hills,	17 Daniel O. Gehr,
6 John M Broomall,	18 Samuel Calvin,
7 James W. Fuller,	19 Edgar Cowan,
8 Levi B Smith,	20 William McKennan,
9 Francis W. Christ,	21 John M Kirkpatrick,
10 David Mumma, Jr.,	22 James Kerr.
11 David Taggart,	23 Richard P. Roberts,
12 Thomas R. Hull,	24 Henry Souther,

25 John Greer,

FOR GOVERNOR,

HON. ANDREW G. CURTIN,

OF CENTRE COUNTY.

FOR CONGRESS—XXIst DISTRICT,

JAMES K. MOORHEAD.

FOR CONGRESS—XXIId DISTRICT.

ROBERT McKNIGHT.

Assembly,

KENNEDY MARSHALL, Pittsburgh.

THOMAS WILLIAMS, Allegheny.

CHARLES L. GOEHRING, Reserve.

WILLIAM DOUGLAS, Elizabeth

ALEXANDER H. BURNS, Findley.

Clerk of the Courts,

WILLIAM A. HERRON, Pitt.

Register,

WILLIAM J. RICHARDSON, Temperanceville.

Recorder,

JONATHAN P. ROSS, Allegheny,

Commissioner,

GEORGE HAMILTON, Pittsburgh.

Auditor,

BENNETT LAKE, Elizabeth.

Surveyor,

O. McGOWAN, Pittsburgh.

Director of the Poor,

HENRY CHALFANT, Wilkins.

OURIER.
STLE, IND.

WALTON P. GOODE, - - - Editor
THURSDAY, OCTOBER 4, 1860.

Republican Ticket.

For President,
ABRAHAM LINCOL
OF ILLINOIS.
For Vice President,
HANNIBAL HAMLI
OF MAINE.

For Governor,
HENRY S. LANE, of Montgomery.
For Lieutenant Governor,
OLIVER P. MORTON, of Wayne.
For Secretary of State,
WILLIAM A. PEELLE, of Randolph.
For Treasurer of State,
JONATHAN S. HARVEY, of Clarke.
For Auditor of State,
ALBERT LANGE, of Vigo.
For Attorney General,
[illegible] J[illegible]ES, of [illegible]burgh.
For Repo[illegible]er of Supreme Court,
BENJAMIN HARRISON, of Marion.
For Clerk of Supreme Court,
JOHN P. JONES, of Lagrang
For Supt. of Public Instruction
MILES J. FLETCHER, of Putnam

For Congress—Fifth District,
GEORGE W. JULIAN.

For Judge of Common Pleas Court,
WILLIAM GROSE.
For District Attorney,
WILLIAM R. HOUGH.

County Ticket.
For Senator—J. H. MELLETT.
For Representative—M. L. BUNDY
For Treasurer—ENSLEY JULIAN.
For Sheriff—JOHN W. VANCE.
For Commissioner—M. F. EDWARDS
For Surveyor—J. M. CLEMENTS.
For Coroner—WM. McDOWELL

For Assessor, Henry Township,
HARVEY W. ALEXANDER

BALLOTS
DRAWER 9
ELECTION-

HELPED ELECT LINCOLN

Republican Ticket.

FOR PRESIDENT,

ABRAHAM LINCOLN,

OF ILLINOIS.

FOR VICE PRESIDENT,

HANNIBAL HAMLIN,

OF MAINE.

Electors for President and Vice President of the United States.

FREDERICK HASSAUREK, of Hamilton County.
JOSEPH M. ROOT, of Erie County.

1st District—		BENJAMIN EGGLESTON.
2d	"	WILLIAM M. DICKSON.
3d	"	FRANK McWHINNEY.
4th	"	JOHN RILEY KNOX.
5th	"	DRESDEN W. H. HOWARD.
6th	"	JOHN M. KELLUM.
7th	"	NELSON RUSH.
8th	"	ABRAHAM THOMSON.
9th	"	JOHN E. HENKLE.
10th	"	HEZEKIAH S. BUNDY.
11th	"	DANIEL B. STEWART.
12th	"	RICHARD P. L. BABER.
13th	"	JOHN BEATTY.
14th	"	WILLARD SLOCUM.
15th	"	JOSEPH ANKENY.
16th	"	EDWARD BALL.
17th	"	JOHN A. DAVENPORT.
18th	"	WILLIAM K. UPHAM.
19th	"	SAMUEL B. PHILBRICK.
20th	"	GEORGE W. BROOKE.
[illegible]		NORMAN K. MACKENZIE.

—Associated Press.

This Republican ballot was cast for Abraham Lincoln in 1860. It is the property of Dr. Paul Moore of Cleveland, who received it from his father, David, who came into possession of the ballot when he was only 10 years old. Notice the name of the first presidential elector—Frederick Hassaurek of Hamilton County.

BALLOTS

DRAWER 9

ELECTION - 860

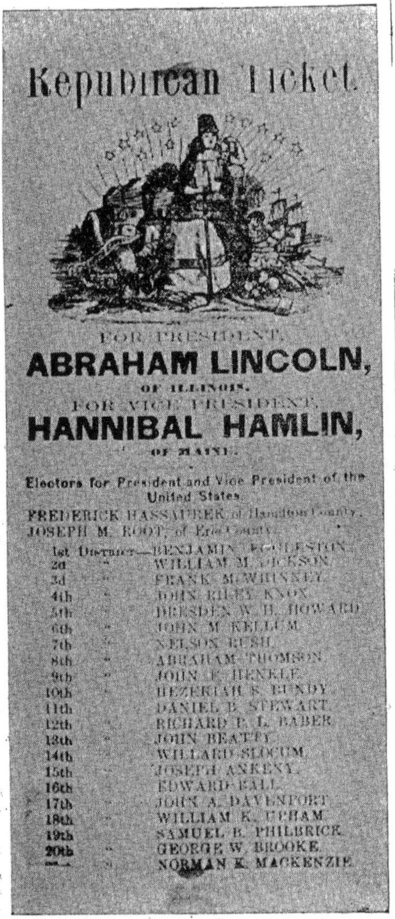

Republican Ticket

FOR PRESIDENT,

ABRAHAM LINCOLN,

OF ILLINOIS.

FOR VICE PRESIDENT,

HANNIBAL HAMLIN,

OF MAINE.

Electors for President and Vice President of the United States.

FREDERICK HASSAUREK, of Hamilton County.
JOSEPH M. ROOT, of Erie County.

1st	District—	BENJAMIN EGGLESTON.
2d	"	WILLIAM M. DICKSON.
3d	"	FRANK McWHINNEY.
4th	"	JOHN RILEY KNOX.
5th	"	DRESDEN W. H. HOWARD.
6th	"	JOHN M. KELLUM.
7th	"	NELSON RUSH.
8th	"	ABRAHAM THOMSON.
9th	"	JOHN F. HENKLE.
10th	"	HEZEKIAH S. BUNDY.
11th	"	DANIEL B. STEWART.
12th	"	RICHARD P. L. BABER.
13th	"	JOHN BEATTY.
14th	"	WILLARD SLOCUM.
15th	"	JOSEPH ANKENY.
16th	"	EDWARD BALL.
17th	"	JOHN A. DAVENPORT.
18th	"	WILLIAM K. UPHAM.
19th	"	SAMUEL B. PHILBRICK.
20th	"	GEORGE W. BROOKE.
[illegible]	"	NORMAN K. MACKENZIE.

AP-Gazette Wirephoto

CLEVELAND, Feb. 12.—This ballot helped elect Lincoln. It was cast in 1860 and is the property of Dr. Paul G. Moore, who received it from his father. The latter acquired it when he was a boy.

This Helped Elect Honest Abe

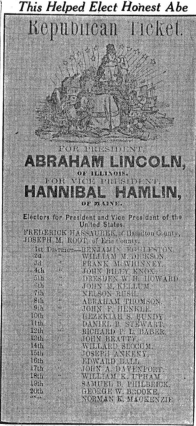

Republican Ticket.

FOR PRESIDENT,

ABRAHAM LINCOLN,

OF ILLINOIS.

FOR VICE PRESIDENT,

HANNIBAL HAMLIN,

OF MAINE.

Electors for President and Vice President of the United States.

FREDERICK HASSAUREK, of Hamilton County,
JOSEPH M. ROOT, of Erie County.

1st District—BENJAMIN EGGLESTON.
2d " WILLIAM M. DICKSON.
3d " FRANK McWHINNEY.
4th " JOHN RILEY KNOX.
5th " DRESDEN W. H. HOWARD.
6th " JOHN M. KELLUM.
7th " NELSON RUSH.
8th " ABRAHAM THOMSON.
9th " JOHN F. HENKLE.
10th " HEZEKIAH S. BUNDY.
11th " DANIEL B. STEWART.
12th " RICHARD P. L. BABER.
13th " JOHN BEATTY.
14th " WILLARD SLOCUM.
15th " JOSEPH ANKENY.
16th " EDWARD BALL.
17th " JOHN A. DAVENPORT.
18th " WILLIAM K. UPHAM.
19th " SAMUEL B. PHILBRICK.
20th " GEORGE W. BROOKE.
21st " NORMAN K. MACKENZIE.

This is a ballot cast for Abraham Lincoln in 1860. It hangs in the office of Dr. Paul G. Moore in the Republic Building. The ballot was given to Dr. Moore by his father, David R. Moore, who got it when he was 10 and living at Reading, O., a suburb of Cincinnati. How the ballot escaped the fire to which such things usually are consigned is not known. But here it is—a vote for Abraham Lincoln and the G. O. P.

to keep California in the Union was led by David Broderick and Alexander Campbell. Campbell was elected Judge of the Twelfth District Court and to the State Assembly, which was allowed under the old California constitution but not possible under present constitution. California was kept in the Union by a bare majority. Judge Alexander Campbell was the father of John B. T. Campbell, present managing editor of The Herald and Express. Lincoln was elected, California remained in the Union, the Civil War came, Broderick was killed in a duel with David Terry, leader of the Southern faction in California, and Judge Campbell presided for a number of years over the Twelfth District Court consisting of the counties of San Francisco, Alameda, Marin and Sonoma.

Nov. 6. —1860— Election.

Republican Ticket.

FOR PRESIDENT,

ABRAHAM LINCOLN.

FOR VICE-PRESIDENT,

HANNIBAL HAMLIN.

FOR ELECTORS,

CHAS. A. WASHBURN, WM. H. WEEKS,
ANTONIO MARIA PICO, CHAS. A. TUTTLE.

LEGISLATIVE TICKET.

For State Senators,

JAMES McM. SHAFTER,
CALEB BURBANK.

For Assemblymen,

S. S. TILTON, ROBERT CLARK,
JOHN W. CHERRY, ALEX. CAMPBELL,
ALVAN FLANDERS, JAMES A. BANKS,
G. E. TITTEL, O. F. WILLEY.

(The successful ticket)

People's Ticket.

Judge of Twelfth District Court,

ALEXANDER CAMPBELL.

District Attorney,

NATHAN PORTER.

President of the Board of Supervisors,

H. F. TESCHEMACHER.

[illegible]

[illegible]

Auditor,

HENRY M. HALE.

Public Administrator,

ADOLPHUS HOLLUB.

Police Judge,

SAMUEL COWLES.

Chief of Police,

MARTIN J. BURKE.

Assessor,

THOMAS TENNENT.

Superintendent of Streets and Highways

GEORGE T. BOHEN.

38472.

Indiana Ballot Of Lincoln Election In 1860 Uncovered In Deep South

By CARROLL LEWIS WILSON
Special Star Correspondent

Winter Park, Fla., Feb. 5—One hundred and forty years after Abraham Lincoln was born near Hodgensville, Ky., a genuine Republican Lincoln ballot of the national election of 1860 has been uncovered here in the deep South. It belongs to Mrs. Esther Burton Conn, formerly of Crothersville, Ind., who now lives in Winter Park.

The ballot was the original property of her great-grandfather, John Brown Lewis, also a native Kentuckian. Like Lincoln, he moved with his family across the Ohio River to Illinois where he enlisted in the Union Army in 1860, the fateful year "Honest Abe" was elected 16th President of the United States, the year of secession and the formation of the Confederate States of America, the eve of four years of Civil War.

THE REDISCOVERED BALLOT is an Indiana state ballot of the Republican ticket. A woodcut of Lincoln with the inscription "Honest Abe" heads it with an eagle astride two crossed American flags. There were 33 stars in the flag of 1860 but the wood-engraver stamped his stars at random and probably guessed at the number. In old-fashioned hand-set type is Republican Ticket. For President, Abraham Lincoln, of Illinois. For Vice-President, Hannibal Hamlin, of Maine. In smaller type is the Presidential Electoral Ticket, the names and counties of two electors of the state at large and 11 district electors.

When he was 15 years old, Frank Burton, deceased brother of the present owner, Mrs. Conn, found the ballot in his grandmother's attic trunk, a fact duly recorded on the back of the ballot by the grandmother in 1921. The Burtons then lived in Bloomingdale, Ind. They later moved to Crothersville, where Mrs. Conn's mother still resides.

ESTHER BURTON was a 16-year-old pupil in Crothersville High School when assigned to write an essay on Abraham Lincoln. Brother Frank gave her his Lincoln ballot on which she based her essay. She put the ballot among her souvenirs which she brought to Florida years later when she married John A. Conn Jr. of Clermont and Winter Park.

Mrs. Conn never showed the ballot to anyone until recently when she found it among her childhood treasures and casually showed it to her husband. Photographs and description were sent to the Library of Congress in Washington and to Dr. Douglas Southall Freeman, editor of the Richmond (Va.) News-Leader, author and authority on Civil War history. These authorities said it is an authentic ballot of the 1860 election.

CAREFULLY PRESERVED, the ballot's print is clear and the paper is not yellowed with age. It still retains a salmon shade, was probably pink. At that time political parties printed their own ballots, each party using a ballot of different color because many voters then could not read, but could easily distinguish colors. When voting, the "ticket," or ballot, was handed to or selected from its pile by the voter, who then marched to the polls and dropped his colored ballot in the proper box in plain view of everybody. This method also insured when a vote was "bought" that "the goods were delivered" in the buyer's presence.

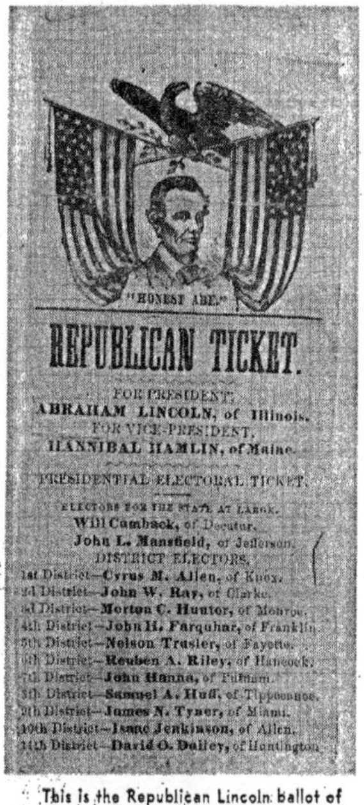

"HONEST ABE."

REPUBLICAN TICKET.

FOR PRESIDENT,
ABRAHAM LINCOLN, of Illinois.
FOR VICE-PRESIDENT,
HANNIBAL HAMLIN, of Maine.

PRESIDENTIAL ELECTORAL TICKET.

ELECTORS FOR THE STATE AT LARGE.
Will Cumback, of Decatur.
John L. Mansfield, of Jefferson.
DISTRICT ELECTORS.
1st District—Cyrus M. Allen, of Knox.
2d District—John W. Ray, of Clarke.
3d District—Morton C. Huntor, of Monroe.
4th District—John H. Farquhar, of Franklin.
5th District—Nelson Trusler, of Fayette.
6th District—Reuben A. Riley, of Hancock.
7th District—John Hanna, of Putnam.
8th District—Samuel A. Huff, of Tippecanoe.
9th District—James N. Tyner, of Miami.
10th District—Isaac Jenkinson, of Allen.
11th District—David O. Dailey, of Huntington.

This is the Republican Lincoln ballot of the national election of 1860 which has been uncovered in Florida.

Slavery was the dominant issue in the 1860 election. During the historic Lincoln-Stephen Douglas debates, Lincoln stated the issue in these memorable words: "'A house divided against itself cannot stand.' I believe this government cannot endure permanently half slave and half free. I do not expect the Union to be dissolved—I do not expect the house to fall—but I do expect that it will cease to be divided. It will become all one thing or all the other."

Thus spoke the man whose leadership helped make it possible for a girl from Indiana to marry a boy from Florida and bring her "damnyankee" ballot to the deepest portion of the deep South, a ballot to which her Southern in-laws today point with unconcealed pride.

TURNING BACK THE CLOCK

BY FRANK Y. GRAYSON

Republican Ticket.

FOR PRESIDENT,
ABRAHAM LINCOLN,
OF ILLINOIS,
FOR VICE PRESIDENT,
HANNIBAL HAMLIN,
OF MAINE.

Electors for President and Vice President of the United States.

FREDERICK HASSAUREK, of Hamilton County.
JOSEPH M. ROOT, of Erie County.

1st District—BENJAMIN EGGLESTON.
2d " WILLIAM M. DICKSON.
3d " FRANK McWHINNEY.
4th " JOHN RILEY KNOX.
5th " DRESDEN W. H. HOWARD.
6th " JOHN M. KELLUM.
7th " NELSON RUSH.
8th " ABRAHAM THOMSON.
9th " JOHN F. HENKLE.
10th " HEZEKIAH S. BUNDY.
11th " DANIEL B. STEWART.
12th " RICHARD P. L. BABER.
13th " JOHN BEATTY.
14th " WILLARD SLOCUM.
15th " JOSEPH ANKENY.
16th " EDWARD BALL.
17th " JOHN A. DAVENPORT.
18th " WILLIAM K. UPHAM.
19th " SAMUEL B. PHILBRICK.
20th " GEORGE W. BROOKE.
21st " NORMAN K. MACKENZIE.

REGULAR NATIONAL DEMOCRATIC NOMINATIONS.

For President,
STEPHEN A. DOUGLAS.
For Vice President,
HERSCHEL V. JOHNSON.

Presidential Electoral Ticket.

SERAPHIM MEYER, of Stark County.
WILLIAM B. WOODS, of Licking.

WILLIAM J. FLAGG, of Hamilton.
JOHN SCHIFF, of Hamilton.
JACOB H. FOOS, of Preble.
SILAS B. WALKER, of Shelby.
EDWARD SHEFFIELD, of Henry.
NEWTON A. DEVORE, of Brown.
HENRY C. COFFMAN, of Fayette.
GEORGE F. STAYMAN, of Delaware.
CHESTER R. MOTT, of Wyandotte.
JOHN D. JAMES, ot Jackson.
JAMES M. MILLER, of Meigs.
SAMUEL G. FOSTER, of Franklin.
WILLIAM DURBIN, of Erie.
BURR KELLOGG, of Ashland.
NICHOLAS F. JOSS, of Holmes.
AMOS LAYMAN, of Washington.
WILSON S. KENNON, of Belmont.
ISRAEL E. CARTER, of Summit.
CHARLES D. ADAMS, of Lake.
GEORGE A. HOWARD, of Ashtabula.
GEORGE WEBSTER, of Jefferson.

—Courtesy Joseph M. Whiteford, 705 South Ridgeland Avenue, Oak Ridge, Ill.

The gentleman who submitted these sample ballots for the famous Lincoln-Douglas election in 1860 has in his possession much Lincolniana and he would like to hear from anyone who might be interested in the collection, which is of much variety. He also submitted a small ballot containing the names of five prominent Cincinnatians who ran for city trustees in that year.

THE CINCINNATI TIMES-STAR

Je. 1950

Drawer 9 Elect. 1860

June 27, 1950

Mr. Joseph M. Whiteford
703 South Ridgeland Ave.
Oak Ridge, Illinois

Dear Mr. Whiteford:

We have just seen the sample ballots for the Lincoln-Douglas election in the CINCINNATI Times-Star.

Would you kindly advise us of the extent of your collection of Lincolniana and whether or not you are offering items for sale.

Very truly yours,

mm/mm

Secretary to Dr. Warren

DRAWER

Oak Park, Ill,
July 10th., 1950.

Dr. Louis A. Warren,
The Lincoln National Life Foundation,
Fort Wayne, Ind.

Attention: Margaret Moellering.

Dear Madam:-

This will acknowledge your letter of June 27th. in reference to the Abraham Lincoln sample ballots as appeared in the Cincinnati-Times Star of June 20th.

These items are for sale, and I would appreciate an offer for same.

At the present time I have several inquiries regarding these items. However, I would prefer to see them in the proper hands where they would be available for the public, rather than in some private collection.

Your interest is appreciated, regreting the delay as I was on a business trip, I remain,

Respectfully,

J M Whiteford

Correct Address:

Joseph M. Whiteford
705 S. Ridgeland Ave.,
Oak Park, Ill.

DRAWER

HENRY E. HUNTINGTON LIBRARY
AND ART GALLERY

American Presidential Ballots
1840 - 1888

September, 1952

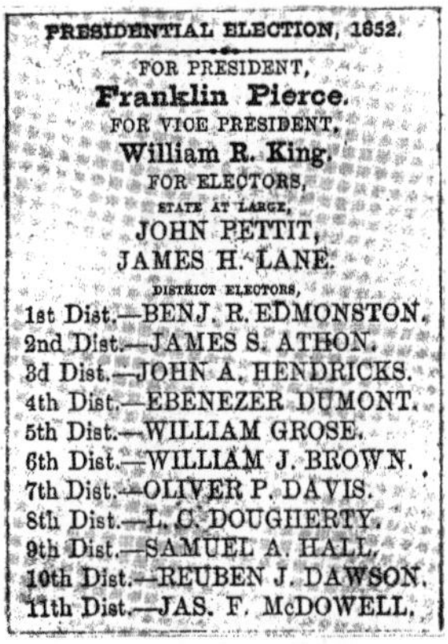
PRESIDENTIAL ELECTION, 1852.
FOR PRESIDENT,
Franklin Pierce.
FOR VICE PRESIDENT,
William R. King.
FOR ELECTORS,
STATE AT LARGE,
JOHN PETTIT,
JAMES H. LANE.
DISTRICT ELECTORS,
1st Dist.—BENJ. R. EDMONSTON.
2nd Dist.—JAMES S. ATHON.
3d Dist.—JOHN A. HENDRICKS.
4th Dist.—EBENEZER DUMONT.
5th Dist.—WILLIAM GROSE.
6th Dist.—WILLIAM J. BROWN.
7th Dist.—OLIVER P. DAVIS.
8th Dist.—L. C. DOUGHERTY.
9th Dist.—SAMUEL A. HALL.
10th Dist.—REUBEN J. DAWSON.
11th Dist.—JAS. F. McDOWELL.

Through the courtesy of Dr. William B. Munro, Vice-Chairman of its Board of Trustees, the Huntington Library is exhibiting during September a portion of his collection of rare American Presidential ballots or tickets used in elections before the days of television, radio, and even today's familiar form of official ballot on which the voter marks his "X".

Until long after the Civil War official ballots were not printed in the United States. Those now exhibited were issued by the various political parties and each bears the names of one party's slate of candidates. Often they contain only the presidential and vice-presidential candidates' names with those of the electors pledged to them; in certain of the later ballots shown, however, the names of the governor, lieutenant-governor, and other state officers appear. Prepared by the party, the ballot was mailed

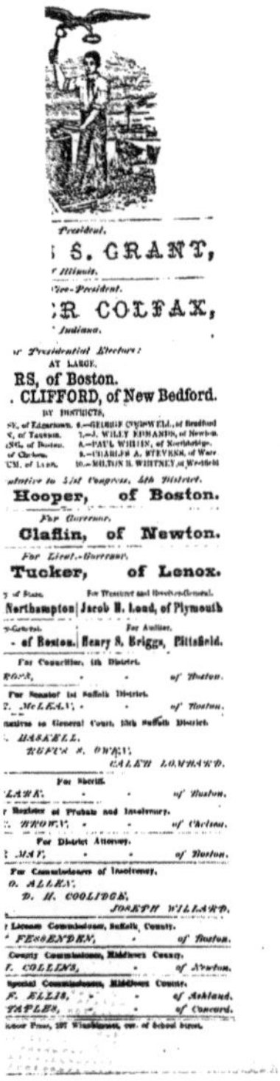

President.
S. GRANT,
Illinois.
Vice-President.
R COLFAX,
Indiana.
Presidential Electors:
AT LARGE.
RS, of Boston.
. CLIFFORD, of New Bedford.
BY DISTRICTS.
Hooper, of Boston.
For Governor.
Claflin, of Newton.
For Lieut.-Governor.
Tucker, of Lenox.
Northampton | Jacob H. Loud, of Plymouth
- of Boston. | Henry S. Briggs, Pittsfield.
HASKELL.
RUFUS S. OWEN,
CALEB LOMBARD.
For Sheriff.
For District Attorney.
For Commissioners of Insolvency.
D. H. COOLIDGE,
JOSEPH WILLARD.
FESSENDEN, of Boston.
COLLINS, of Newton.
ELLIS, of Ashland.
TAPLES, of Concord.

1884

ocratic Party—4,874,986
veland—Thomas A. Hendricks
blican Party—4,851,981
G. Blaine—John A. Logan

th ballots shown offer full slates

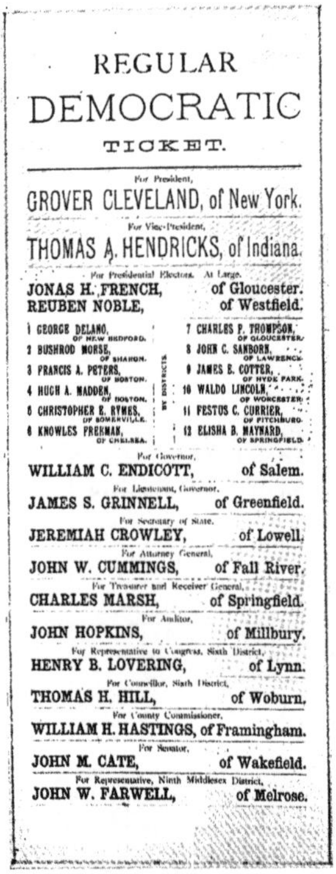

REGULAR
DEMOCRATIC
TICKET.

For President,
GROVER CLEVELAND, of New York.
For Vice-President,
THOMAS A. HENDRICKS, of Indiana.
For Presidential Electors. At Large.
JONAS H. FRENCH, of Gloucester.
REUBEN NOBLE, of Westfield.

BY DISTRICTS.

1 GEORGE DELANO, OF NEW BEDFORD.
2 BUSHROD MORSE, OF SHARON.
3 FRANCIS A. PETERS, OF BOSTON.
4 HUGH A. MADDEN, OF BOSTON.
5 CHRISTOPHER E. RYMES, OF SOMERVILLE.
6 KNOWLES FREEMAN, OF CHELSEA.
7 CHARLES P. THOMPSON, OF GLOUCESTER.
8 JOHN C. SANBORN, OF LAWRENCE.
9 JAMES E. COTTER, OF HYDE PARK.
10 WALDO LINCOLN, OF WORCESTER.
11 FESTUS C. CURRIER, OF FITCHBURG.
12 ELISHA B. MAYNARD, OF SPRINGFIELD.

For Governor,
WILLIAM C. ENDICOTT, of Salem.
For Lieutenant Governor,
JAMES S. GRINNELL, of Greenfield.
For Secretary of State,
JEREMIAH CROWLEY, of Lowell.
For Attorney General,
JOHN W. CUMMINGS, of Fall River.
For Treasurer and Receiver General,
CHARLES MARSH, of Springfield.
For Auditor,
JOHN HOPKINS, of Millbury.
For Representative to Congress, Sixth District,
HENRY B. LOVERING, of Lynn.
For Councillor, Sixth District,
THOMAS H. HILL, of Woburn.
For County Commissioner,
WILLIAM H. HASTINGS, of Framingham.
For Senator,
JOHN M. CATE, of Wakefield.
For Representative, Ninth Middlesex District,
JOHN W. FARWELL, of Melrose.

1888*

Republican Party—5,439,853
Benjamin Harrison—Levi P. Morton

Democratic Party—5,540,329
Grover Cleveland—Allen G. Thurman

*Electoral College vote gave the election to Harrison.

This, one of the last of the old-style ballots, bears the symbolic American eagle and flags and the slogan "Protection to American Industries—the Keystone of National Prosperity."

HENRY E. HUNTINGTON LIBRARY
AND ART GALLERY

American Presidential Ballots 1840-1888

September, 1952

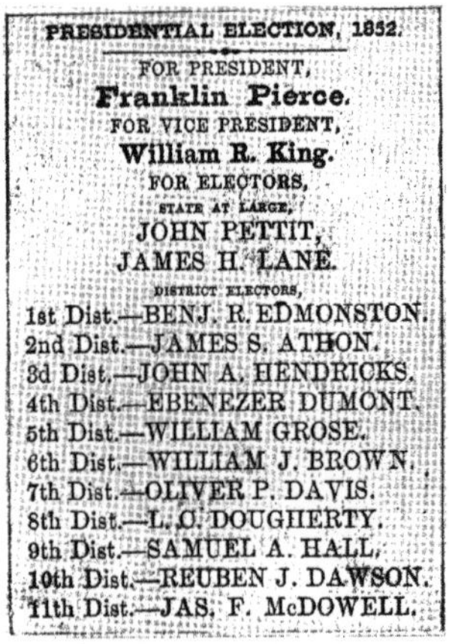

PRESIDENTIAL ELECTION, 1852.
FOR PRESIDENT,
Franklin Pierce.
FOR VICE PRESIDENT,
William R. King.
FOR ELECTORS,
STATE AT LARGE,
JOHN PETTIT,
JAMES H. LANE.
DISTRICT ELECTORS,
1st Dist.—BENJ. R. EDMONSTON.
2nd Dist.—JAMES S. ATHON.
3d Dist.—JOHN A. HENDRICKS.
4th Dist.—EBENEZER DUMONT.
5th Dist.—WILLIAM GROSE.
6th Dist.—WILLIAM J. BROWN.
7th Dist.—OLIVER P. DAVIS.
8th Dist.—L. C. DOUGHERTY.
9th Dist.—SAMUEL A. HALL.
10th Dist.—REUBEN J. DAWSON.
11th Dist.—JAS. F. McDOWELL.

Through the courtesy of Dr. William B. Munro, Vice-Chairman of its Board of Trustees, the Huntington Library is exhibiting during September a portion of his collection of rare American Presidential ballots or tickets used in elections before the days of television, radio, and even today's familiar form of official ballot on which the voter marks his "X".

Until long after the Civil War official ballots were not printed in the United States. Those now exhibited were issued by the various political parties and each bears the names of one party's slate of candidates. Often they contain only the presidential and vice-presidential candidates' names with those of the electors pledged to them; in certain of the later ballots shown, however, the names of the governor, lieutenant-governor, and other state officers appear. Prepared by the party, the ballot was mailed to the voter or thrust into his hands by the party agents when he approached the polling booth. This practice made it easy to "stuff the ballot box" since a dishonest person could deposit more than one ballot in the box. No strict count was kept of the used and unused ballots. There was no "X" mark; the "ticket" was merely dropped into the box, or, in some cases, was first signed on the back by the voter. Note for example the ballot of 1860 bearing the name of Breckenridge for President, on which is printed "Write your name on the back of this ticket." If the voter wished to vote the "straight ticket," he used the ballot as it was; if any of the candidates did not please him, he might "scratch the ticket" by crossing out names and substituting others.

It was not until the late 1880's that the so-called Australian ballot came into somewhat general use. At first it was termed by the politicians, somewhat derisively, the "Kangaroo ballot." It was the first American ballot requiring the voter to mark a cross, but its most distinguishing feature is that it was *official,* printed by the election authorities and not by the political parties. Since the advent of the Australian ballot, these tickets ceased to be available to collectors because all ballots are strictly guarded until the election results are officially declared after both used and unused ballots have been fully accounted for. Then, when the recount period has expired, they are destroyed.

The portion of Dr. Munro's collection now being shown at the Library includes American presidential ballots dating from 1840 to 1888. At least one ballot from every presidential election between those dates is exhibited. The earliest is one which was used to cast a vote for Martin Van Buren in 1840. A few of the elections are represented by ballots for both the winning and losing candidates. A rare example of the ballot naming Jefferson Davis as the unopposed candidate for the presidency of the Confederate States of America is also included.

The ballots shown in the exhibition are listed below in chronological order. For each election, the winning party, the popular vote, and the winning President and Vice-President are listed, followed by the defeated party or parties with their votes and candidates.

1840

Whig Party—1,275,017
William H. Harrison—John Tyler
Democratic Party—1,128,702
Martin Van Buren—Richard M. Johnson

Van Buren and Johnson headed a winning ticket in 1836 but were defeated by "Tippecanoe and Tyler too" in 1840. Note the name of the elector for the 15th District on this ticket has been "scratched" and a new name written in. This may mean that the original nominee had died or declined to serve, or merely that the voter who used this ballot didn't want to vote for him.

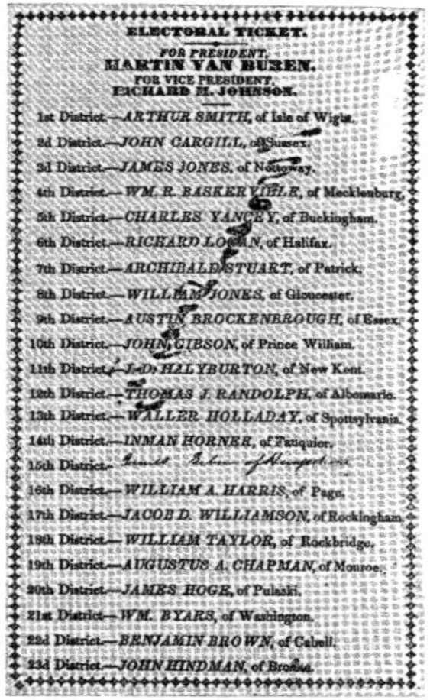
ELECTORAL TICKET.
FOR PRESIDENT,
MARTIN VAN BUREN.
FOR VICE PRESIDENT,
RICHARD M. JOHNSON.
1st District.—ARTHUR SMITH, of Isle of Wight.
2d District.—JOHN CARGILL, of Sussex.
3d District.—JAMES JONES, of Nottoway.
4th District.—WM. R. BASKERVILLE, of Mecklenburg.
5th District.—CHARLES YANCEY, of Buckingham.
6th District.—RICHARD LOGAN, of Halifax.
7th District.—ARCHIBALD STUART, of Patrick.
8th District.—WILLIAM JONES, of Gloucester.
9th District.—AUSTIN BROCKENBROUGH, of Essex.
10th District.—JOHN GIBSON, of Prince William.
11th District.—J. D. HALYBURTON, of New Kent.
12th District.—THOMAS J. RANDOLPH, of Albemarle.
13th District.—WALLER HOLLADAY, of Spottsylvania.
14th District.—INMAN HORNER, of Fauquier.
15th District.—[illegible]
16th District.—WILLIAM A. HARRIS, of Page.
17th District.—JACOB D. WILLIAMSON, of Rockingham.
18th District.—WILLIAM TAYLOR, of Rockbridge.
19th District.—AUGUSTUS A. CHAPMAN, of Monroe.
20th District.—JAMES HOGE, of Pulaski.
21st District.—WM. BYARS, of Washington.
22d District.—BENJAMIN BROWN, of Cabell.
23d District.—JOHN HINDMAN, of Brooke.

1844

Democratic Party—1,337,243
James K. Polk—George M. Dallas
Whig Party—1,299,062
Henry Clay—Theodore Frelinghuysen

This election was held on Monday, November 4, instead of on the customary Tuesday.

1848

Whig Party—1,360,099
Zachary Taylor—Millard Fillmore
Democratic Party—1,220,544
Lewis Cass—William O. Butler

This "People's ticket" contains the names of two Presidents. Taylor died in office and was succeeded by Fillmore.

1852

Democratic Party—1,601,474
Franklin Pierce—William R. King
Whig Party—1,386,580
Winfield Scott—William A. Graham

No party name or symbol distinguishes this ticket.

1856

Democratic Party—1,838,169
James Buchanan—John C. Breckenridge
Republican Party—1,341,264
John C. Fremont—William L. Dayton
Whig Party—874,534
Millard Fillmore—Andrew J. Donelson

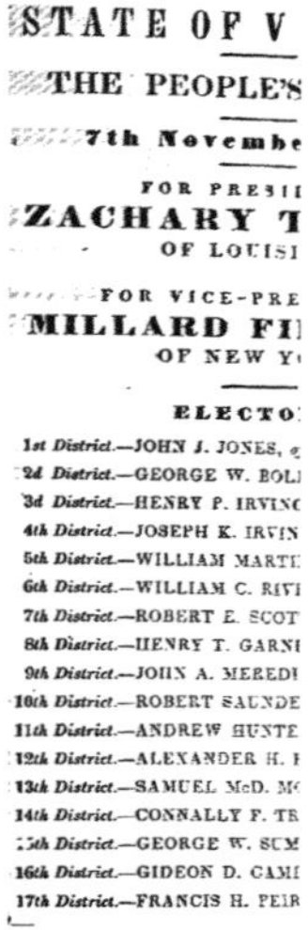
STATE OF V
THE PEOPLE'S
7th Novembe
FOR PRESI
ZACHARY T
OF LOUISI
FOR VICE-PRE
MILLARD FI
OF NEW Y
ELECTO
1st District.—JOHN J. JONES,
2d District.—GEORGE W. BOL
3d District.—HENRY P. IRVIN
4th District.—JOSEPH K. IRVIN
5th District.—WILLIAM MART
6th District.—WILLIAM C. RIV
7th District.—ROBERT E. SCOT
8th District.—HENRY T. GARN
9th District.—JOHN A. MERED
10th District.—ROBERT SAUNDE
11th District.—ANDREW HUNTE
12th District.—ALEXANDER H.
13th District.—SAMUEL McD. M
14th District.—CONNALLY F. TR
15th District.—GEORGE W. SUM
16th District.—GIDEON D. CAM
17th District.—FRANCIS H. PEIR

This ballot was designed wi the voter by its "eye appeal." two candidates and the "stylis influence the wavering voter.

1860

Republican Party—
Abraham Lincoln—Ha
Democratic Party—
Stephen A. Douglas—He
Southern Democratic P
John C. Breckenridge—
Constitutional Union P
John Bell—Edwa

The cut of Abraham Linco ballot shows him clean shaven in 1861, however, he had gr he wore for the rest of his li name of the Quaker poet, Joh among the list of presidential el

1864

Republican Party—
Abraham Lincoln—An
Democratic Party—
George B. McClellan—Ge
The Republican ballot of h

to the voter or thrust into his hands by the party agents when he approached the polling booth. This practice made it easy to "stuff the ballot box" since a dishonest person could deposit more than one ballot in the box. No strict count was kept of the used and unused ballots. There was no "X" mark; the "ticket" was merely dropped into the box, or, in some cases, was first signed on the back by the voter. Note for example the ballot of 1860 bearing the name of Breckenridge for President, on which is printed "Write your name on the back of this ticket." If the voter wished to vote the "straight ticket," he used the ballot as it was; if any of the candidates did not please him, he might "scratch the ticket" by crossing out names and substituting others.

It was not until the late 1880's that the so-called Australian ballot came into somewhat general use. At first it was termed by the politicians, somewhat derisively, the "Kangaroo ballot." It was the first American ballot requiring the voter to mark a cross, but its most distinguishing feature is that it was *official*, printed by the election authorities and not by the political parties. Since the advent of the Australian ballot, these tickets ceased to be available to collectors because all ballots are strictly guarded until the election results are officially declared after both used and unused ballots have been fully accounted for. Then, when the recount period has expired, they are destroyed.

The portion of Dr. Munro's collection now being shown at the Library includes American presidential ballots dating from 1840 to 1888. At least one ballot from every presidential election between those dates is exhibited. The earliest is one which was used to cast a vote for Martin Van Buren in 1840. A few of the elections are represented by ballots for both the winning and losing candidates. A rare example of the ballot naming Jefferson Davis as the unopposed candidate for the presidency of the Confederate States of America is also included.

The ballots shown in the exhibition are listed below in chronological order. For each election, the winning party, the popular vote, and the winning President and Vice-President are listed, followed by the defeated party or parties with their votes and candidates.

1840

Whig Party—1,275,017
William H. Harrison—John Tyler
Democratic Party—1,128,702
Martin Van Buren—Richard M. Johnson

Van Buren and Johnson headed a winning ticket in 1836 but were defeated by "Tippecanoe and Tyler too" in 1840. Note the name of the elector for the 15th District on this ticket has been "scratched" and a new name written in. This may mean that the original nominee had died or declined to serve, or merely that the voter who used this ballot didn't want to vote for him.

ELECTORAL TICKET.
FOR PRESIDENT,
MARTIN VAN BUREN.
FOR VICE PRESIDENT,
RICHARD M. JOHNSON.
1st District.—ARTHUR SMITH, of Isle of Wight.
2d District.—JOHN CARGILL, of Sussex.
3d District.—JAMES JONES, of Nottoway.
4th District.—WM. R. BASKERVILLE, of Mecklenburg.
5th District.—CHARLES YANCEY, of Buckingham.
6th District.—RICHARD LOGAN, of Halifax.
7th District.—ARCHIBALD STUART, of Patrick.
8th District.—WILLIAM JONES, of Gloucester.
9th District.—AUSTIN BROCKENBROUGH, of Essex.
10th District.—JOHN GIBSON, of Prince William.
11th District.—J. D. HALYBURTON, of New Kent.
12th District.—THOMAS J. RANDOLPH, of Albemarle.
13th District.—WALLER HOLLADAY, of Spottsylvania.
14th District.—INMAN HORNER, of Fauquier.
15th District.—
16th District.—WILLIAM A. HARRIS, of Page.
17th District.—JACOB D. WILLIAMSON, of Rockingham.
18th District.—WILLIAM TAYLOR, of Rockbridge.
19th District.—AUGUSTUS A. CHAPMAN, of Monroe.
20th District.—JAMES HOGE, of Pulaski.
21st District.—WM. BYARS, of Washington.
22d District.—BENJAMIN BROWN, of Cabell.
23d District.—JOHN HINDMAN, of Brooke.

1844

Democratic Party—1,337,243
James K. Polk—George M. Dallas
Whig Party—1,299,062
Henry Clay—Theodore Frelinghuysen

This election was held on Monday, November 4, instead of on the customary Tuesday.

1848

Whig Party—1,360,099
Zachary Taylor—Millard Fillmore
Democratic Party—1,220,544
Lewis Cass—William O. Butler

This "People's ticket" contains the names of two Presidents. Taylor died in offiee and was succeeded by Fillmore.

1852

Democratic Party—1,601,474
Franklin Pierce—William R. King
Whig Party—1,386,580
Winfield Scott—William A. Graham

No party name or symbol distinguishes this ticket.

1856

Democratic Party—1,838,169
James Buchanan—John C. Breckenridge
Republican Party—1,341,264
John C. Fremont—William L. Dayton
Whig Party—874,534
Millard Fillmore—Andrew J. Donelson

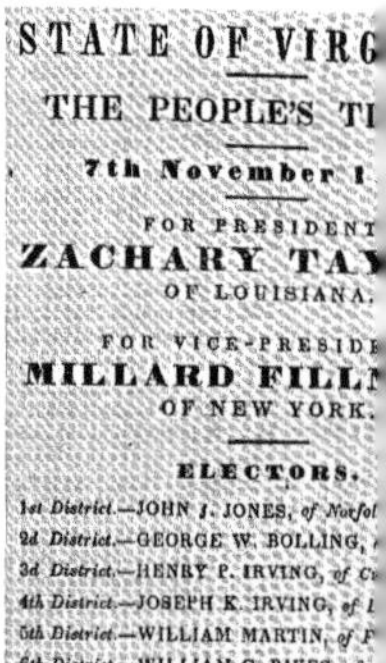

STATE OF VIRG
THE PEOPLE'S TI
7th November 1
FOR PRESIDENT
ZACHARY TA
OF LOUISIANA.
FOR VICE-PRESIDE
MILLARD FILL
OF NEW YORK.
ELECTORS.
1st District.—JOHN J. JONES, of Norfol
2d District.—GEORGE W. BOLLING,
3d District.—HENRY P. IRVING, of C
4th District.—JOSEPH K. IRVING, of
5th District.—WILLIAM MARTIN, of
6th District.—WILLIAM C. RIVES, of
7th District.—ROBERT E. SCOTT, of
8th District.—HENRY T. GARNETT, of
9th District.—JOHN A. MEREDITH, of
10th District.—ROBERT SAUNDERS, of
11th District.—ANDREW HUNTER, of
12th District.—ALEXANDER H. H. STU
13th District.—SAMUEL McD. MOORE,
14th District.—CONNALLY F. TRIGG,
15th District.—GEORGE W. SUMMERS,
16th District.—GIDEON D. CAMDEN, of
17th District.—FRANCIS H. PEIRPOINT

This ballot was designed with a
the voter by its "eye appeal." The
two candidates and the "stylish" ty
influence the wavering voter.

1860

Republican Party—1,86
Abraham Lincoln—Hanniba
Democratic Party—1,37
Stephen A. Douglas—Herschel
Southern Democratic Party—
John C. Breckenridge—Jose
Constitutional Union Party—
John Ball—Edward Eve

The cut of Abraham Lincoln on
ballot shows him clean shaven. By
in 1861, however, he had grown
he wore for the rest of his life. N
name of the Quaker poet, John G.
among the list of presidential electors

1864

Republican Party—2,213
Abraham Lincoln—Andrew
Democratic Party—1,802
George B. McClellan—George
The Republican ballot of this year

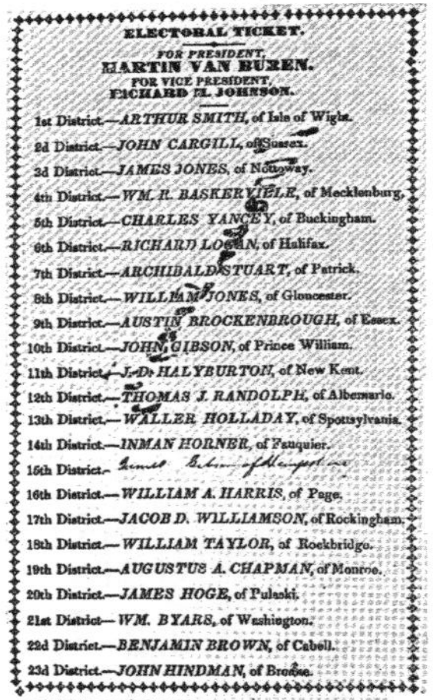
ELECTORAL TICKET.
FOR PRESIDENT,
MARTIN VAN BUREN.
FOR VICE PRESIDENT,
RICHARD M. JOHNSON.
1st District.—ARTHUR SMITH, of Isle of Wight.
2d District.—JOHN CARGILL, of Sussex.
3d District.—JAMES JONES, of Nottoway.
4th District.—WM. R. BASKERVILLE, of Mecklenburg.
5th District.—CHARLES YANCEY, of Buckingham.
6th District.—RICHARD LOGAN, of Halifax.
7th District.—ARCHIBALD STUART, of Patrick.
8th District.—WILLIAM JONES, of Gloucester.
9th District.—AUSTIN BROCKENBROUGH, of Essex.
10th District.—JOHN GIBSON, of Prince William.
11th District.—J. D. HALYBURTON, of New Kent.
12th District.—THOMAS J. RANDOLPH, of Albemarle.
13th District.—WALLER HOLLADAY, of Spottsylvania.
14th District.—INMAN HORNER, of Fauquier.
15th District.—
16th District.—WILLIAM A. HARRIS, of Page.
17th District.—JACOB D. WILLIAMSON, of Rockingham.
18th District.—WILLIAM TAYLOR, of Rockbridge.
19th District.—AUGUSTUS A. CHAPMAN, of Monroe.
20th District.—JAMES HOGE, of Pulaski.
21st District.—WM. BYARS, of Washington.
22d District.—BENJAMIN BROWN, of Cabell.
23d District.—JOHN HINDMAN, of Brooke.

1844
Democratic Party—1,337,243
James K. Polk—George M. Dallas
Whig Party—1,299,062
Henry Clay—Theodore Frelinghuysen

This election was held on Monday, November 4, instead of on the customary Tuesday.

1848
Whig Party—1,360,099
Zachary Taylor—Millard Fillmore
Democratic Party—1,220,544
Lewis Cass—William O. Butler

This "People's ticket" contains the names of two Presidents. Taylor died in office and was succeeded by Fillmore.

1852
Democratic Party—1,601,474
Franklin Pierce—William R. King
Whig Party—1,386,580
Winfield Scott—William A. Graham

No party name or symbol distinguishes this ticket.

1856
Democratic Party—1,838,169
James Buchanan—John C. Breckenridge
Republican Party—1,341,264
John C. Fremont—William L. Dayton
Whig Party—874,534
Millard Fillmore—Andrew J. Donelson

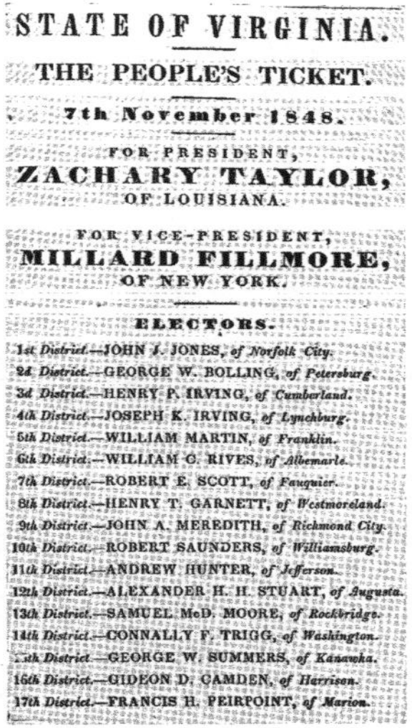
STATE OF VIRGINIA.
THE PEOPLE'S TICKET.
7th November 1848.
FOR PRESIDENT,
ZACHARY TAYLOR,
OF LOUISIANA.
FOR VICE-PRESIDENT,
MILLARD FILLMORE,
OF NEW YORK.
ELECTORS.
1st District.—JOHN J. JONES, of Norfolk City.
2d District.—GEORGE W. BOLLING, of Petersburg.
3d District.—HENRY P. IRVING, of Cumberland.
4th District.—JOSEPH K. IRVING, of Lynchburg.
5th District.—WILLIAM MARTIN, of Franklin.
6th District.—WILLIAM C. RIVES, of Albemarle.
7th District.—ROBERT E. SCOTT, of Fauquier.
8th District.—HENRY T. GARNETT, of Westmoreland.
9th District.—JOHN A. MEREDITH, of Richmond City.
10th District.—ROBERT SAUNDERS, of Williamsburg.
11th District.—ANDREW HUNTER, of Jefferson.
12th District.—ALEXANDER H. H. STUART, of Augusta.
13th District.—SAMUEL McD. MOORE, of Rockbridge.
14th District.—CONNALLY F. TRIGG, of Washington.
15th District.—GEORGE W. SUMMERS, of Kanawha.
16th District.—GIDEON D. CAMDEN, of Harrison.
17th District.—FRANCIS H. PEIRPOINT, of Marion.

This ballot was designed with a view of attracting the voter by its "eye appeal." The portraits of the two candidates and the "stylish" types were used to influence the wavering voter.

1860
Republican Party—1,866,452
Abraham Lincoln—Hannibal Hamlin
Democratic Party—1,376,957
Stephen A. Douglas—Herschel V. Johnson
Southern Democratic Party—849,781
John C. Breckenridge—Joseph Lane
Constitutional Union Party—588,879
John Ball—Edward Everett

The cut of Abraham Lincoln on the Republican ballot shows him clean shaven. By inauguration day in 1861, however, he had grown the beard which he wore for the rest of his life. Note also that the name of the Quaker poet, John G. Whittier, appears among the list of presidential electors.

1864
Republican Party—2,213,665
Abraham Lincoln—Andrew Johnson
Democratic Party—1,802,237
George B. McClellan—George H. Pendleton

The Republican ballot of this year lists a full slate

of candidates while its Democratic counterpart leav it to the discretion of the voter to write in his ow candidate for five county offices.

1868
Republican Party—3,012,833
Ulysses S. Grant—Schuyler Colfax
Democratic Party—2,703,249
Horatio Seymour—Francis P. Blair, Jr.

Both the Republican and Democratic parties offere a full slate of candidates on these ballots for 1868.

1872
Republican Party—3,597,132
Ulysses S. Grant—Henry Wilson
Democratic Party—2,834,125
Horace Greeley—B. Gratz Brown

The woodcut on this Republican ballot suggest a platform of peace and prosperity.

1876*
Republican Party—4,033,950
Rutherford B. Hayes—William A. Wheeler
Democratic Party—4,284,885
Samuel J. Tilden—Thomas A. Hendricks
*Decided by Electoral Commission in favor of Hayes

The simple form of the earlier ballots is indicate by this Republican ballot which lists only th presidential and vice-presidential candidates.

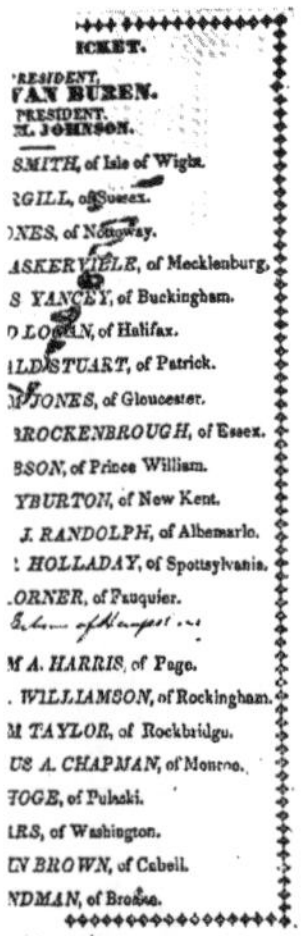

ICKET.

RESIDENT,
VAN BUREN.
PRESIDENT,
M. JOHNSON.

SMITH, of Isle of Wight.
RGILL, of Sussex.
ONES, of Nottoway.
ASKERVILLE, of Mecklenburg.
S YANCEY, of Buckingham.
D LOGAN, of Halifax.
ALD STUART, of Patrick.
M JONES, of Gloucester.
BROCKENBROUGH, of Essex.
BSON, of Prince William.
YBURTON, of New Kent.
J. RANDOLPH, of Albemarle.
HOLLADAY, of Spottsylvania.
ORNER, of Fauquier.
M A. HARRIS, of Page.
WILLIAMSON, of Rockingham.
M TAYLOR, of Rockbridge.
US A. CHAPMAN, of Monroe.
TOGE, of Pulaski.
IRS, of Washington.
EN BROWN, of Cabell.
NDMAN, of Brooke.

1844

: Party—1,337,243
k—George M. Dallas
'arty—1,299,062
Theodore Frelinghuysen
eld on Monday, November 4,
omary Tuesday.

1848

'arty—1,360,099
or—Millard Fillmore
: Party—1,220,544
—William O. Butler
it" contains the names of two
d in office and was succeeded

1852

c Party—1,601,474
ce—William R. King
Party—1,386,580
—William A. Graham
or symbol distinguishes this

1856

ic Party—1,838,169
n—John C. Breckenridge
n Party—1,341,264
ont—William L. Dayton
Party—874,534
re—Andrew J. Donelson

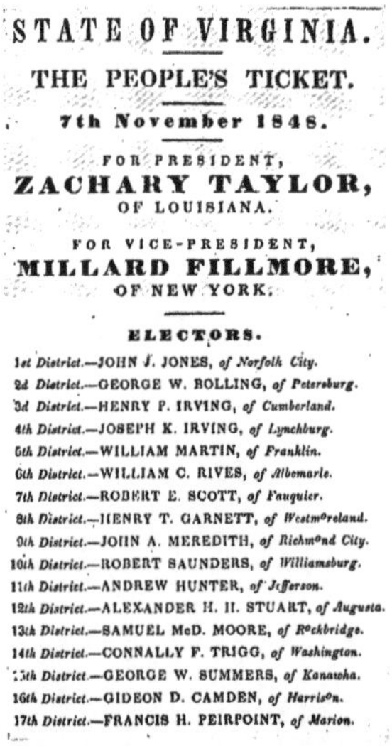

STATE OF VIRGINIA.

THE PEOPLE'S TICKET.

7th November 1848.

FOR PRESIDENT,
ZACHARY TAYLOR,
OF LOUISIANA.

FOR VICE-PRESIDENT,
MILLARD FILLMORE,
OF NEW YORK.

ELECTORS.

1st District.—JOHN J. JONES, of Norfolk City.
2d District.—GEORGE W. BOLLING, of Petersburg.
3d District.—HENRY P. IRVING, of Cumberland.
4th District.—JOSEPH K. IRVING, of Lynchburg.
5th District.—WILLIAM MARTIN, of Franklin.
6th District.—WILLIAM C. RIVES, of Albemarle.
7th District.—ROBERT E. SCOTT, of Fauquier.
8th District.—HENRY T. GARNETT, of Westmoreland.
9th District.—JOHN A. MEREDITH, of Richmond City.
10th District.—ROBERT SAUNDERS, of Williamsburg.
11th District.—ANDREW HUNTER, of Jefferson.
12th District.—ALEXANDER H. H. STUART, of Augusta.
13th District.—SAMUEL McD. MOORE, of Rockbridge.
14th District.—CONNALLY F. TRIGG, of Washington.
15th District.—GEORGE W. SUMMERS, of Kanawha.
16th District.—GIDEON D. CAMDEN, of Harrison.
17th District.—FRANCIS H. PEIRPOINT, of Marion.

This ballot was designed with a view of attracting the voter by its "eye appeal." The portraits of the two candidates and the "stylish" types were used to influence the wavering voter.

1860

Republican Party—1,866,452
Abraham Lincoln—Hannibal Hamlin
Democratic Party—1,376,957
Stephen A. Douglas—Herschel V. Johnson
Southern Democratic Party—849,781
John C. Breckenridge—Joseph Lane
Constitutional Union Party—588,879
John Ball—Edward Everett

The cut of Abraham Lincoln on the Republican ballot shows him clean shaven. By inauguration day in 1861, however, he had grown the beard which he wore for the rest of his life. Note also that the name of the Quaker poet, John G. Whittier, appears among the list of presidential electors.

1864

Republican Party—2,213,665
Abraham Lincoln—Andrew Johnson
Democratic Party—1,802,237
George B. McClellan—George H. Pendleton

The Republican ballot of this year lists a full slate

DEMOCRATIC TICKET

Our Principles

FOR PRESIDENT
JAMES BUCHANAN
of Pennsylvania
FOR VICE PRESIDENT
JOHN C. BRECKINRIDGE
of Kentucky

ELECTORS

1st District E. W. MASSENBURG of Portsmouth.
2d do. THOMAS H. CAMPBELL of Nottoway.
3d do. A. HUGHES DILLARD of Henry.
4th do. JAMES GARLAND of Campbell.
5th do. JOHN GOODE, Jr. of Bedford.
6th do. ALEX. JONES of Chesterfield.
7th do. WM. B. TALIAFERRO of Gloucester.
8th do. R. L. MONTAGUE of Middlesex.
9th do. JAMES BARBOUR of Culpeper.
10th do. J. RANDOLPH TUCKER of Frederick.
11th do. JOHN T. HARRIS of Rockingham.
12th do. A. G. PENDLETON of Giles.
13th do. JOHN B. FLOYD of Washington.
14th do. SAMUEL L. HAYS of Gilmer.
15th do. SHERRARD CLEMENS of Ohio.

Write your Name on the back of the Ticket

Election on Tuesday November 4th 1856.

of candidates while its Democratic counterpart leaves it to the discretion of the voter to write in his own candidate for five county offices.

1868

Republican Party—3,012,833
Ulysses S. Grant—Schuyler Colfax
Democratic Party—2,703,249
Horatio Seymour—Francis P. Blair, Jr.

Both the Republican and Democratic parties offered a full slate of candidates on these ballots for 1868.

1872

Republican Party—3,597,132
Ulysses S. Grant—Henry Wilson
Democratic Party—2,834,125
Horace Greeley—B. Gratz Brown

The woodcut on this Republican ballot suggests a platform of peace and prosperity.

1876*

Republican Party—4,033,950
Rutherford B. Hayes—William A. Wheeler
Democratic Party—4,284,885
Samuel J. Tilden—Thomas A. Hendricks
*Decided by Electoral Commission in favor of Hayes.

The simple form of the earlier ballots is indicated by this Republican ballot which lists only the presidential and vice-presidential candidates.

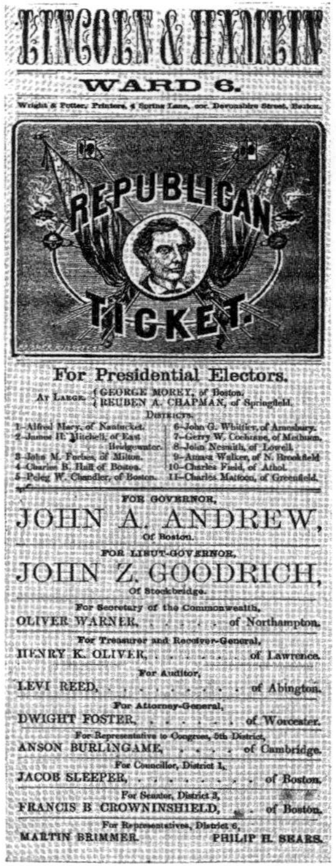
LINCOLN & HAMLIN
WARD 6.
Wright & Potter, Printers, 4 Spring Lane, cor. Devonshire Street, Boston.
REPUBLICAN TICKET.
For Presidential Electors.
At Large. { GEORGE MOREY, of Boston. REUBEN A. CHAPMAN, of Springfield.
Districts.
1–Alfred Macy, of Nantucket.
2–James H. Mitchell, of East Bridgewater.
3–John M. Forbes, of Milton.
4–Charles B. Hall, of Boston.
5–Peleg W. Chandler, of Boston.
6–John G. Whittier, of Amesbury.
7–Gerry W. Cochrane, of Methuen.
8–John Nesmith, of Lowell.
9–Amasa Walker, of N. Brookfield.
10–Charles Field, of Athol.
11–Charles Mattoon, of Greenfield.
FOR GOVERNOR,
JOHN A. ANDREW,
Of Boston.
FOR LIEUT.-GOVERNOR,
JOHN Z. GOODRICH,
Of Stockbridge.
For Secretary of the Commonwealth,
OLIVER WARNER, of Northampton.
For Treasurer and Receiver-General,
HENRY K. OLIVER, of Lawrence.
For Auditor,
LEVI REED, of Abington.
For Attorney-General,
DWIGHT FOSTER, of Worcester.
For Representative to Congress, 5th District,
ANSON BURLINGAME, of Cambridge.
For Councillor, District 1,
JACOB SLEEPER, of Boston.
For Senator, District 3,
FRANCIS B. CROWNINSHIELD, of Boston.
For Representatives, District 6,
MARTIN BRIMMER. PHILIP H. SEARS.

1880

Republican Party—4,454,416
James A. Garfield—Chester A. Arthur

Democratic Party—4,444,952
Winfield S. Hancock—William H. English

Note that this ballot has a notice of copyright below the party name.

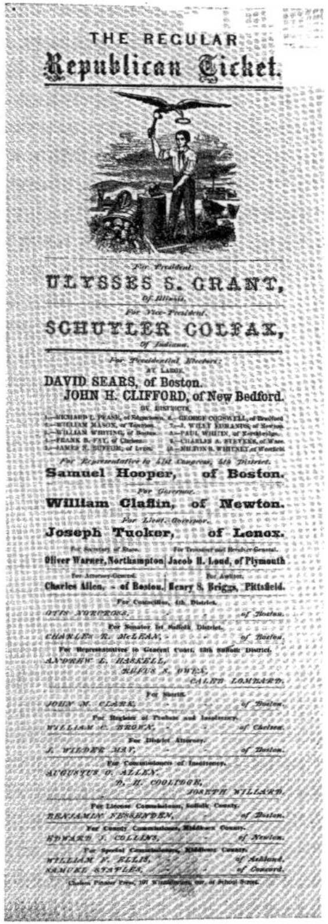
THE REGULAR
Republican Ticket.
For President,
ULYSSES S. GRANT,
Of Illinois.
For Vice-President,
SCHUYLER COLFAX,
Of Indiana.
For Presidential Electors;
At Large.
DAVID SEARS, of Boston.
JOHN H. CLIFFORD, of New Bedford.
For Representative to 41st Congress, 4th District.
Samuel Hooper, of Boston.
For Governor,
William Claflin, of Newton.
For Lieut.-Governor,
Joseph Tucker, of Lenox.
For Secretary of State.
Oliver Warner, Northampton
For Treasurer and Receiver-General.
Jacob H. Loud, of Plymouth
For Attorney-General.
Charles Allen, of Boston.
For Auditor.
Henry S. Briggs, Pittsfield.

1884

Democratic Party—4,874,986
Grover Cleveland—Thomas A. Hendricks
Republican Party—4,851,981
James G. Blaine—John A. Logan

Note that both ballots shown offer full slates of candidates.

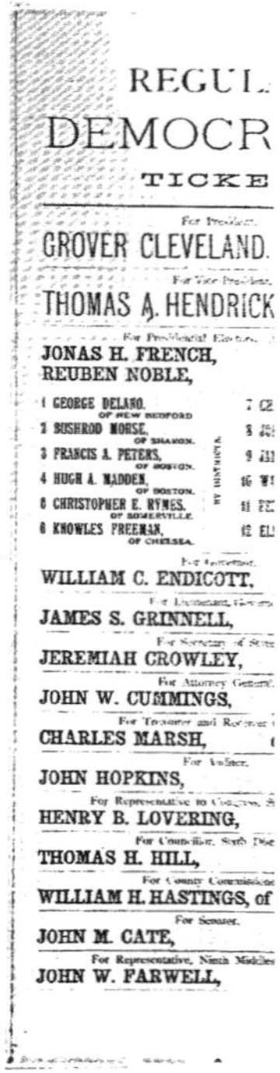
REGUL
DEMOCR
TICKE
For President.
GROVER CLEVELAND.
For Vice President.
THOMAS A. HENDRICK
JONAS H. FRENCH,
REUBEN NOBLE,
1 GEORGE DELANO, OF NEW BEDFORD
2 BUSHROD MORSE, OF SHARON.
3 FRANCIS A. PETERS, OF BOSTON.
4 HUGH A. MADDEN, OF BOSTON.
5 CHRISTOPHER E. RYMES, OF SOMERVILLE.
6 KNOWLES FREEMAN, OF CHELSEA.
BY DISTRICTS.
WILLIAM C. ENDICOTT,
JAMES S. GRINNELL,
JEREMIAH CROWLEY,
JOHN W. CUMMINGS,
CHARLES MARSH,
JOHN HOPKINS,
HENRY B. LOVERING,
THOMAS H. HILL,
WILLIAM H. HASTINGS, of
For Senator.
JOHN M. CATE,
JOHN W. FARWELL,

1888*

Republican Party—5
Benjamin Harrison—Le

Democratic Party—5
Grover Cleveland—Allen

*Electoral College vote gave the

This, one of the last of the ol the symbolic American eagle slogan "Protection to American I stone of National Prosperity."

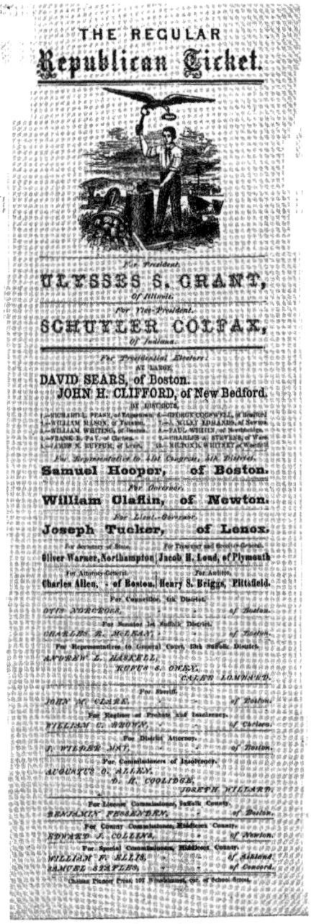

THE REGULAR
Republican Ticket.

For President,
ULYSSES S. GRANT,
of Illinois.
For Vice-President,
SCHUYLER COLFAX,
of Indiana.
For Presidential Electors:
AT LARGE,
DAVID SEARS, of Boston.
JOHN H. CLIFFORD, of New Bedford.
For Representative to 41st Congress, 4th District,
Samuel Hooper, of Boston.
For Governor,
William Claflin, of Newton.
For Lieut.-Governor,
Joseph Tucker, of Lenox.
Oliver Warner, Northampton | Jacob H. Loud, of Plymouth
Charles Allen, of Boston. | Henry S. Briggs, Pittsfield.

1884

Democratic Party—4,874,986
Grover Cleveland—Thomas A. Hendricks
Republican Party—4,851,981
James G. Blaine—John A. Logan

Note that both ballots shown offer full slates of candidates.

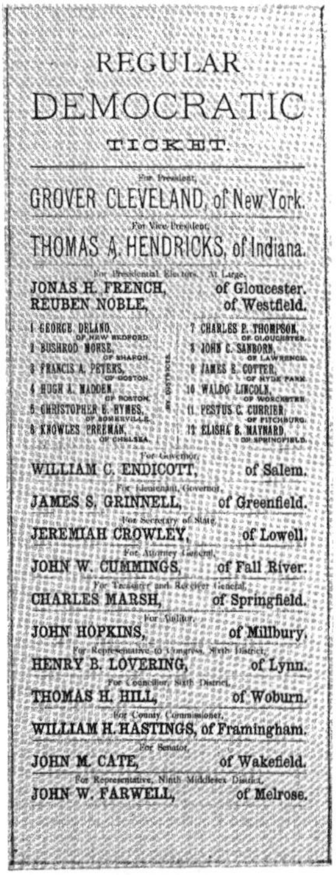

REGULAR
DEMOCRATIC
TICKET.

For President,
GROVER CLEVELAND, of New York.
For Vice President,
THOMAS A. HENDRICKS, of Indiana.
For Presidential Electors. At Large,
JONAS H. FRENCH, of Gloucester.
REUBEN NOBLE, of Westfield.

BY DISTRICTS.
1 GEORGE DELANO, OF NEW BEDFORD.
2 BUSHROD MORSE, OF SHARON.
3 FRANCIS A. PETERS, OF BOSTON.
4 HUGH A. MADDEN, OF BOSTON.
5 CHRISTOPHER E. HYMES, OF SOMERVILLE.
6 KNOWLES FREEMAN, OF CHELSEA.
7 CHARLES P. THOMPSON, OF GLOUCESTER.
8 JOHN C. SANBORN, OF LAWRENCE.
9 JAMES E. COTTER, OF HYDE PARK.
10 WALDO LINCOLN, OF WORCESTER.
11 FESTUS C. CURRIER, OF FITCHBURG.
12 ELISHA B. MAYNARD, OF SPRINGFIELD.

For Governor,
WILLIAM C. ENDICOTT, of Salem.
For Lieutenant Governor,
JAMES S. GRINNELL, of Greenfield.
For Secretary of State,
JEREMIAH CROWLEY, of Lowell.
For Attorney General,
JOHN W. CUMMINGS, of Fall River.
For Treasurer and Receiver General,
CHARLES MARSH, of Springfield.
For Auditor,
JOHN HOPKINS, of Millbury.
For Representative to Congress, Sixth District,
HENRY B. LOVERING, of Lynn.
For Councillor, Sixth District,
THOMAS H. HILL, of Woburn.
For County Commissioner,
WILLIAM H. HASTINGS, of Framingham.
For Senator,
JOHN M. CATE, of Wakefield.
For Representative, Ninth Middlesex District,
JOHN W. FARWELL, of Melrose.

1888*

Republican Party—5,439,853
Benjamin Harrison—Levi P. Morton

Democratic Party—5,540,329
Grover Cleveland—Allen G. Thurman

*Electoral College vote gave the election to Harrison.

This, one of the last of the old-style ballots, bears the symbolic American eagle and flags and the slogan "Protection to American Industries—the Keystone of National Prosperity."

HENRY E. HUNTINC
AND ART G/

American Preside
1840-18

September,

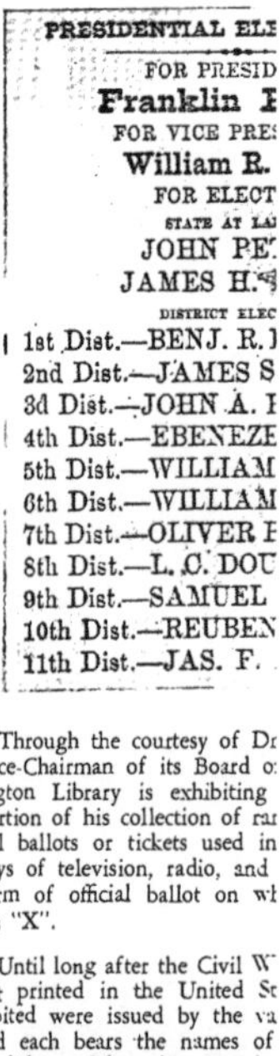

PRESIDENTIAL EL
FOR PRESID
Franklin I
FOR VICE PRES
William R.
FOR ELECT
STATE AT LA
JOHN PE
JAMES H.
DISTRICT ELEC
1st Dist.—BENJ. R.
2nd Dist.—JAMES S
3d Dist.—JOHN A. I
4th Dist.—EBENEZE
5th Dist.—WILLIAM
6th Dist.—WILLIAM
7th Dist.—OLIVER F
8th Dist.—L. C. DOU
9th Dist.—SAMUEL
10th Dist.—REUBEN
11th Dist.—JAS. F.

Through the courtesy of Dr
Vice-Chairman of its Board o
ington Library is exhibiting
portion of his collection of ra
tial ballots or tickets used in
days of television, radio, and
form of official ballot on wh
his "X".

Until long after the Civil W
not printed in the United St
hibited were issued by the va
and each bears the names of
candidates. Often they contain
and vice-presidential candidate
of the electors pledged to the
later ballots shown, however,
governor, lieutenant-governor, a
appear. Prepared by the party,

THE REGULAR

Republican Ticket.

For President,

ULYSSES S. GRANT,

Of Illinois.

For Vice-President.

SCHUYLER COLFAX,

Of Indiana.

For Presidential Electors:

AT LARGE,

DAVID SEARS, of Boston.

JOHN H. CLIFFORD, of New Bedford.

BY DISTRICTS,

1.—RICHARD L. PEASE, of Edgartown. 6.—GEORGE COGSWELL, of Bradford.
2.—WILLIAM MASON, of Taunton. 7.—J. WILEY EDMANDS, of Newton.
3.—WILLIAM WHITING, of Boston. 8.—PAUL WHITIN, of Northbridge.
4.—FRANK B. FAY, of Chelsea. 9.—CHARLES A. STEVENS, of Ware.
5.—JAMES N. BUFFUM, of Lynn. 10.—MILTON B. WHITNEY, of Westfield.

For Representative to 41st Congress, 4th District.

Samuel Hooper, of Boston.

For Governor.

William Claflin, of Newton.

For Lieut.-Governor.

Joseph Tucker, of Lenox.

For Secretary of State.	For Treasurer and Receiver-General.
Oliver Warner, Northampton	**Jacob H. Loud, of Plymouth**
For Attorney-General.	For Auditor.
Charles Allen, - of Boston.	**Henry S. Briggs, Pittsfield.**

For Councillor, 4th District.

OTIS NORCROSS, - - of Boston.

For Senator 1st Suffolk District.

CHARLES R. McLEAN, - - of Boston.

For Representatives to General Court, 13th Suffolk District.

ANDREW L. HASKELL,
RUFUS S. OWEN,
CALEB LOMBARD.

For Sheriff.

JOHN M. CLARK, - - of Boston.

For Register of Probate and Insolvency.

WILLIAM C. BROWN, - - of Chelsea.

For District Attorney.

J. WILDER MAY, - - of Boston.

For Commissioners of Insolvency.

AUGUSTUS O. ALLEN,
D. H. COOLIDGE,
JOSEPH WILLARD.

For License Commissioner, Suffolk County.

BENJAMIN FESSENDEN, - of Boston.

For County Commissioner, Middlesex County.

EDWARD J. COLLINS, - of Newton.

For Special Commissioners, Middlesex County.

WILLIAM F. ELLIS, - - of Ashland.
SAMUEL STAPLES, - - of Concord.

Chelsea Pioneer Press, 107 Winnisimmet, cor. of School Street.

1884

Democratic Party—4,874,986
Grover Cleveland—Thomas A. Hendricks
Republican Party—4,851,981
James G. Blaine—John A. Logan

Note that both ballots shown offer full slates of candidates.

REGULAR

DEMOCRATIC

TICKET.

For President.

GROVER CLEVELAND, of New York.

For Vice President.

THOMAS A. HENDRICKS, of Indiana.

For Presidential Electors, At Large.

JONAS H. FRENCH, of Gloucester.
REUBEN NOBLE, of Westfield.

BY DISTRICTS.

1 GEORGE DELANO, of New Bedford.	7 CHARLES P. THOMPSON, of Gloucester.
2 BUSHROD MORSE, of Sharon.	8 JOHN C. SANBORN, of Lawrence.
3 FRANCIS A. PETERS, of Boston.	9 JAMES E. COTTER, of Hyde Park.
4 HUGH A. MADDEN, of Boston.	10 WALDO LINCOLN, of Worcester.
5 CHRISTOPHER E. RYMES, of Somerville.	11 FESTUS C. CURRIER, of Fitchburg.
6 KNOWLES FREEMAN, of Chelsea.	12 ELISHA B. MAYNARD, of Springfield.

For Governor.

WILLIAM C. ENDICOTT, of Salem.

For Lieutenant Governor.

JAMES S. GRINNELL, of Greenfield.

For Secretary of State.

JEREMIAH CROWLEY, of Lowell.

For Attorney General.

JOHN W. CUMMINGS, of Fall River.

For Treasurer and Receiver General.

CHARLES MARSH, of Springfield.

For Auditor.

JOHN HOPKINS, of Millbury.

For Representative to Congress, Sixth District.

HENRY B. LOVERING, of Lynn.

For Councillor, Sixth District.

THOMAS H. HILL, of Woburn.

For County Commissioner.

WILLIAM H. HASTINGS, of Framingham.

For Senator.

JOHN M. CATE, of Wakefield.

For Representative, Ninth Middlesex District.

JOHN W. FARWELL, of Melrose.

1888*

Republican Party—5,439,853
Benjamin Harrison—Levi P. Morton

Democratic Party—5,540,329
Grover Cleveland—Allen G. Thurman

*Electoral College vote gave the election to Harrison.

This, one of the last of the old-style ballots, bears the symbolic American eagle and flags and the slogan "Protection to American Industries—the Keystone of National Prosperity."

HENRY E. HUNTINGTON LIBRARY
AND ART GALLERY

American Presidential Ballots 1840 - 1888

September, 1952

PRESIDENTIAL ELECTION, 1852.

FOR PRESIDENT,

Franklin Pierce.

FOR VICE PRESIDENT,

William R. King.

FOR ELECTORS,

STATE AT LARGE,

JOHN PETTIT,
JAMES H. LANE.

DISTRICT ELECTORS,

1st Dist.—BENJ. R. EDMONSTON.
2nd Dist.—JAMES S. ATHON.
3d Dist.—JOHN A. HENDRICKS.
4th Dist.—EBENEZER DUMONT.
5th Dist.—WILLIAM GROSE.
6th Dist.—WILLIAM J. BROWN.
7th Dist.—OLIVER P. DAVIS.
8th Dist.—L. C. DOUGHERTY.
9th Dist.—SAMUEL A. HALL.
10th Dist.—REUBEN J. DAWSON.
11th Dist.—JAS. F. McDOWELL.

Through the courtesy of Dr. William B. Munr Vice-Chairman of its Board of Trustees, the Hun ington Library is exhibiting during September portion of his collection of rare American Preside tial ballots or tickets used in elections before tl days of television, radio, and even today's famili form of official ballot on which the voter mark his "X".

Until long after the Civil War official ballots wer not printed in the United States. Those now e hibited were issued by the various political partie and each bears the names of one party's slate o candidates. Often they contain only the presidentia and vice-presidential candidates' names with thos of the electors pledged to them; in certain of th later ballots shown, however, the names of th governor, lieutenant-governor, and other state officer appear. Prepared by the party, the ballot was maile

EXHIBITS BALLOT HERE WHICH WAS USED IN DAYS OF LINCOLN

An official ballot, which helped elect Abraham Lincoln president in 1860 was brought to The Evening Tribune office today by John Hancock, visiting in the city from Santa Barbara.

This document, approximately six inches long by two and a-half wide, bears the names of Samuel Brannan, Sacramento; J. G. McCallum, San Jose; W. W. Crane, Alameda; Charles C. McClay, Santa Clara, and Warner Oliver, Siskiyou. All these men were candidates for election to the state assembly.

William Higby of Calveras sought election to congress on this ballot, and O. H. Burnham of Sonora, aspired to the job of supervisor for the 3rd district.

In addition proposition on the ballot was the proposal to increase the capital stock of the Placerville and Sacramento railway by $100,000.

According to Hancock the ballot box, containing the document he carries, was on a bullion stage, driven by his father, James Hancock, when it was held up between Sonora and Sacramento. In the attempted robbery the elder Hancock is reported to have slain two bandits.

Hancock contemplates placing the document for which he has been offered $1000, on exhibition here.

DRAWER 9 E

Lightning Source UK Ltd.
Milton Keynes UK
UKHW021132090219
336936UK00008B/1181/P

9 780260 457257